WG

Old-Time Country Wisdom

Old-Time Country Wisdom

A Celebration of Good Old-Fashioned Common Sense

Compiled and Edited by Criswell Freeman

WALNUT GROVE PRESS
Nashville, TN 37205

ISBN 1-887655-26-3

The ideas expressed in this book are not, in all cases, exact quotations, as some have been edited for clarity and brevity. In all cases, the author has attempted to maintain the speaker's original intent. In some cases, material for this book was obtained from secondary sources, primarily print media. While every effort was made to ensure the accuracy of these sources, the accuracy cannot be guaranteed. For additions, deletions, corrections or clarifications in future editions of this text, please write WALNUT GROVE PRESS.

Printed in the United States of America
Cover Design by Mary Mazer
Typesetting & Page Layout by Sue Gerdes
Editor for Walnut Grove Press: Alan Ross
1 2 3 4 5 6 7 8 9 10 • 97 98 99 00 01

ACKNOWLEDGMENTS
The author gratefully acknowledges the helpful support of Angela Beasley, Dick and Mary Freeman, Mary Susan Freeman, and Jim Gallery.

For Sam and Angie Knight

Old-Time Country Wisdom at Its Best

Table of Contents

Introduction

I was raised in a family whose roots were sunk deep into the soil of the rural South. My parents and grandparents were proud of their heritage, and they handed down that pride to us kids. Along with their history lessons, the family elders taught us something even more important: common sense.

Each day, or so it seemed, a grown-up would stop to share a little sermon about life. My father was the sermonizer-in-chief. Dad lectured on the fear of God, the dignity of hard work, and the value of a dollar. He taught us to respect our elders and to help our neighbors. He demanded honesty, courtesy and dignity — or else!

Naturally, we youngsters had little interest in my father's sermonettes, or anyone else's for that matter. But we listened politely (because we knew what was good for us). And over time, a strange thing happened: In spite of ourselves, we learned.

This book is a collection of sayings and quotations that reflect the old-fashioned common sense of rural America. Quoted sources include patriots, philosophers, preachers, humorists, and of course, the founding father of American practicality, Ben Franklin.

Old-time country wisdom is as timely and fresh today as it was a hundred years ago because common sense, like good fatherly advice, never goes out of style.

1

Old-Time Advice

In the country, common-sense advice is as plentiful as dandelion seeds on a windy spring day. Simply ask an old-timer a question or two, and soon the wisdom will begin to flow like an everlasting spring. Your job is simple: listen and learn.

Listening to advice is easy, but following it can be hard. As Josh Billings once observed, "Advice is like castor oil — easy to give but dreadful to take."

In this chapter, we consider the medicinal properties of old-time country wisdom. The most important lessons of life are sometimes distasteful. But like castor oil, old-fashioned common sense is good for what ails you.

He that won't be counseled can't be helped.

Poor Richard's Almanac

If wisdom's ways you wisely seek, five things
observe with care: of whom you speak,
to whom you speak, and how and when
and where.

The Old Farmer's Almanac, 1851

Praise in public. Correct in private.

Old-Time Saying

After-advice is fool's advice.

Old-Time Saying

What the poor need is less advice
and more helping hands.

Old-Time Saying

Look up and not down.
Look forward and not back.
Look out and not in,
and lend a hand.

Edward Everett Hale

Never speak ill of the dead.

Old-Time Saying

Take things always by the smooth handle.

Thomas Jefferson

Don't jump from the frying pan into the fire.

Old-Time Saying

Observe all men; thyself most.

Poor Richard's Almanac

Take your own advice; you'll be too busy
to bore others with it.

Old-Time Saying

Tell me my faults, and mend your own.

Poor Richard's Almanac

Never neglect the opportunity of keeping
your mouth shut.

The Missouri Pharmacist

Better slip with foot than tongue.

Poor Richard's Almanac

Silence is the hardest argument to refute.

Josh Billings

A closed mouth catches no flies.

Old-Time Saying

It's no good arguing with the inevitable.

James Russell Lowell

All good abides with him who waiteth wisely.

Henry David Thoreau

There's absolutely no reason for being rushed along with the rush. Everybody should be free to go very slow.

Robert Frost

Haste makes waste.

Poor Richard's Almanac

Be like a postage stamp — stick to one thing until you get there.

Josh Billings

Cultivate only the habits
that you are willing should master you.

Elbert Hubbard

Too many cooks spoil the soup.

Old-Time Saying

Do not wait for a rainy day to fix your roof.

Old-Time Saying

Oversee your workmen. If they be boys,
separate them; for it is true: one boy is a boy,
two boys are a half a boy; but three boys
are no boy at all.

The Old Farmer's Almanac

Tie two or three ol' horses to a good one
and take off down the road.

Lawton Brooks

Don't buy a pig in a poke.

Old-Time Saying

Don't bite the hand that feeds you.

Old-Time Saying

Now I believe in feedin' whatever you have.
Buy poor, feed him fat.... Everybody wants
a pretty, fat horse.

Horse Trader's Advice

Fools need advice most, but wise men only
are the better for it.

Poor Richard's Almanac

Ask advice, but use your own common sense.

Old-Time Saying

2

Common Sense

It is often said that, "A handful of common sense is worth a bushel full of learning." Today, education is available to all, but wisdom remains in short supply. It seems that the modern-day harvest of common sense is far from a bumper crop.

In this chapter, we examine the bountiful rewards of down-to-earth, level-headed judgment. And we acknowledge the fact that there is nothing very common about common sense.

A fool is someone who doesn't know
that he doesn't know.

Old-Time Saying

It's better to know nothing than to know
what isn't so.

Josh Billings

He's a fool that cannot conceal his wisdom.

Poor Richard's Almanac

The bigger a man's head is, the easier it is
to fill his shoes.

Old-Time Saying

The best way to convince a fool that
he is wrong is to let him have his own way.

Josh Billings

Some people go the wrong way down
a one-way street, then get mad
when you don't follow!

Mike Cook

Be neither silly nor cunning, but wise.

Poor Richard's Almanac

An investment in knowledge always pays
the best interest.

Ben Franklin

A child's education should begin at least
a hundred years before he is born.

Oliver Wendell Holmes, Sr.

The philosophy of one century
is the common sense of the next.

Henry Ward Beecher

At 20 years of age the will reigns;
at 30 the wit, at 40 the judgment.

Poor Richard's Almanac

The doors of wisdom are never shut.

Poor Richard's Almanac

School days, school days,
    Dear old golden-rule days,
    Readin' and 'ritin' and 'rithmetic,
    Taught to the tune of a hick'ry stick.

Will D. Cobb, 1907

It were happy if we studied nature more
    in natural things and acted according
    to nature whose rules are few, plain,
        and more reasonable.

William Penn

Reason often makes mistakes,
    but the conscience never does.

Josh Billings

There are lazy minds as well as lazy bodies.
Poor Richard's Almanac

Great good-nature, without prudence,
is a great misfortune.
Poor Richard's Almanac

A narrow mind has a broad tongue.
Old-Time Saying

There is one thing about hens that looks
like wisdom — they don't cackle much
till they've laid their eggs.
Josh Billings

A little education is a dangerous thing.
Old-Time Saying

You can't judge a book by its cover.
Old-Time Saying

Experience keeps a dear school,
yet fools will learn in no other.
Poor Richard's Almanac

One thorn of experience is worth
a whole wilderness of warning.
James Russell Lowell

Never let the same dog bite you twice.
Old-Time Saying

Common sense is the rarest thing in the world and the most valuable.

Old-Time Saying

3

Happiness

William Penn advised, "Seek not to be rich, but happy." This advice is particularly appropriate for anyone who earns his living from the land. While country life has countless rewards, quick monetary gain is not among them.

On the pages that follow, we chart a course on the road to happiness. That road, while not paved with gold, is available to all who earnestly seek it. Furthermore, it goes right through the middle of the countryside.

Don't mistake pleasure
for happiness.

Josh Billings

Happiness is a habit. Cultivate it.

Elbert Hubbard

Talk happiness. The world is sad enough
without your woe.

Ella Wheeler Wilcox

When I whittle, I forget everything;
don't nothing bother me.

John Arnold

Just the thought of a plan to go to town
on Saturday was the source of great joy
and anticipation.

Roy Webster

Dislike what deserves it, but never hate.

William Penn

Happiness is a perfume you can't pour
on others without getting a few drops
on yourself.

Ralph Waldo Emerson

Happiness is where you find it.

Old-Time Saying

Nothing is certain except death and taxes.

Old-Time Saying

Write on your heart that every day is the best day of the year.

Ralph Waldo Emerson

We find in life exactly what we put in.
Ralph Waldo Emerson

Life is a great bundle of little things.
Oliver Wendell Holmes, Sr.

In youth the absence of pleasure is pain;
in old age the absence of pain is pleasure.
The Old Farmer's Almanac, 1892

A long life may not be good enough,
but a good life is long enough.
Poor Richard's Almanac

Every man's life is a plan of God.

Horace Bushnell

As in a game of cards, so in the game of life,
we must play what is dealt to us; and the
glory consists not so much in winning,
as in playing a poor hand well.

Josh Billings

Life is a preparation for the future;
and the best preparation for the future
is to live as if there were none.

Elbert Hubbard

The best way to prepare for life
is to begin to live.

Elbert Hubbard

Keep trying to win; keep playing the game; but always keep room in your heart for a song.

Grantland Rice

You've got to continue to grow, or you're just like last night's cornbread — stale and dry.

Loretta Lynn

Avarice and happiness never saw each other,
how then should they become acquainted?
Poor Richard's Almanac

Money will buy everything but happiness.
Old-Time Saying

Wealth is not his that has it,
but his that enjoys it.
Poor Richard's Almanac

4

The Good Earth

In 1620, Sir Francis Bacon, a city-dwelling philosopher, wrote, "Nature, to be commanded, must be obeyed." Almost two centuries later, Ralph Waldo Emerson observed, "The first farmer was the first man; and all historic nobility rests on possession and use of the land." Both men were right. From the beginning of civilization, the foundation of human enterprise has depended, in large part, upon the intelligent utilization of the land. Today, little has changed.

On the pages that follow, we consider the splendor and majesty of Mother Nature. She is a generous parent — so long as we obey her rules.

Those who labor in the earth
      are the chosen people of God.

Thomas Jefferson

To own a bit of ground, to scratch it with a
hoe, to plant seeds, and watch their renewal
of life — this is the commonest delight of the
race, the most satisfactory thing a man can do.

Charles Dudley Warner

If Eden be on earth at all, 'tis that which
      we the country call.

Henry Vaughan

Remember that agriculture is the best
    of culture, and he that follows the plowing
      is engaged in an employment
       that would not disgrace a king.

The Old Farmer's Almanac, 1836

Overplanted fields make a rich father
but a poor son. Every bit taken from the earth
    must be returned, or it suffers.

1778 Almanac

Blessed be agriculture! if one does not have too much of it.

Charles Dudley Warner

One is nearer God's heart
in a garden than
anywhere else
on earth.

Dorothy Frances Gurney

No occupation is so delightful to me
as the culture of the earth, and no culture
comparable to that of the garden.

Thomas Jefferson

Eventually, a gardener becomes
a philosopher.

Barbara Dodge Borland

A garden is a thing of beauty
and a job forever.

Richard Briers

In order to live off the garden,
you practically have to live in it.

Kin Hubbard

It is difficult to think anything but pleasant
thoughts while eating a homegrown tomato.

Lewis Grizzard

Man must go back to nature for information.

Thomas Paine

We do not see nature with our eyes,
but with our understandings and our hearts.

William Hazlitt

When I first open my eyes upon the morning
meadows and look out upon the beautiful
world, I thank God I am alive.

Ralph Waldo Emerson

Day's sweetest moments are at dawn.

Ella Wheeler Wilcox

After breathing the lived-in air of the
farmhouse all winter, it is good to inhale the
new smell of the outdoors and the clean body
of the earth.

Eric Sloane

Nature is painting for us, day after day,
pictures of infinite beauty if only we have
the eyes to see them.

John Ruskin

There is something about sun and soil
that heals broken bodies and jangled nerves.

Nature Magazine, February, 1946

The landscape belongs to the man
who looks at it.

Ralph Waldo Emerson

Country life does not always have breadth,
but it has depth. It is neither artificial nor
superficial but is kept close to realities.

Calvin Coolidge

You don't live longer in the country.
It just seems that way.

Dick Syatt

Never lose an opportunity of seeing anything
that is beautiful; for beauty is God's handwriting
— a wayside sacrament.

Ralph Waldo Emerson

See Nature, and through her, God.

Henry David Thoreau

Consider the lilies of the field, how they grow;
they toil not, neither do they spin: and yet I say
unto you, that even Solomon in all his glory
was not arrayed like one of these.

Matthew 6: 28, 29

There's a church in the valley by the wildwood,
no lovelier place in the dale;
no spot is so dear to my childhood
as the little brown church in the vale.
O come, come, come, come, come to the church
in the wildwood, O come to the church
in the dale. No spot is so dear to my childhood
as the little brown church in the vale.

William S. Pitts, 1864

5

Family

In 1887, *The Farmer's Almanac* warned, "Always leave home with a tender good-bye and loving words. They may be the last." Certainly this advice held true for city-dwellers and country folk alike, but the Old-Time farmer had a special reason for fostering harmony in the clan: good labor relations.

In the good old days, a farmer with a big congenial family enjoyed a distinct economic advantage: lots of free help. Farm families worked together, played together, and prayed together. Hard. The close-knit family was as much a part of the country tradition as dirt roads and home cookin'. Thankfully, in many homes — on the farm and off — the tradition lives on.

Next to God, thy parents.

William Penn

There is no friendship, no love,
like that of the parent for the child.

Henry Ward Beecher

Reverence and cherish your parents.

Thomas Jefferson

I can recall the gentle squeaking of the
white-painted porch swing blending with the
soft, soothing harmonies of mother's hymns,
as clearly as if it were yesterday.

Marilyn Kluger

If you would be loved, love and be lovable.

Poor Richard's Almanac

You can build a house,
but you have to make a home.

Old-Time Saying

It takes a heap o' lovin' in a house
to make it a home.

Edgar A. Guest

You haven't lived if you haven't loved.

Old-Time Saying

If you marry for money,
        you'll earn every penny.
Old-Time Saying

You can bear your own faults, and why not
        a fault in your wife?
Poor Richard's Almanac

Love looks through a telescope,
        envy through a microscope.
Josh Billings

A good wife and health
        is a man's best wealth.
Poor Richard's Almanac

A man without a wife is but half a man.
Poor Richard's Almanac

All men are different.
All husbands are
the same.

Old-Time Saying

Treat your wife with respect,
   that thy children may also.
       The Old Farmer's Almanac, 1809

Children are the farmer's richest blessing
and, when trained in the habits of industry,
they become the best members of society
    when they grow into life.
        Farmer's Manual

If a person is industrious and so fortunate
as to have a family capable of joining in his
labors and living in the bonds of affection,
there can be no doubt that he will prosper.
        James Pickering

Teach your child to hold his tongue,
   he'll learn fast enough to speak.
       Poor Richard's Almanac

I made a deal with my kids. If they'd do nothing to embarrass me, I'd do nothing to embarrass them. It worked out fine.

Andy Devine

Keep your family from the abominable practice of backbiting.

The Old Farmer's Almanac, 1811

6

Neighbors

In the country, even strangers wave to each other as they pass. And neighbors still help neighbors. This spirit of cooperation is more than a tradition; it's a necessity because big jobs require lots of helping hands. Good neighbors often supply the hands.

Ralph Waldo Emerson noted, "The only way to have a friend is to be one." It might be added that the only way to have a good neighbor is to be one. In this chapter, you'll learn how.

Neighbors

I shall pass through life but once.
Let me show kindness now as I shall not pass
this way again.

William Penn

Scatter seeds of kindness.

George Ade

When befriended, remember it.
When you befriend, forget it.

Poor Richard's Almanac

In life, you can never do a kindness
too soon because you never know how soon
it will be too late.

Ralph Waldo Emerson

If you can make people kind, not merely
respectable, the problem will be solved.

Elbert Hubbard

Let bygones be bygones.

Old-Time Saying

Folks never understand the folks they hate.

James Russell Lowell

Love your enemies, for they tell you
your faults.

Poor Richard's Almanac

We awaken in others the same attitude
of mind we hold toward them.

Elbert Hubbard

Hear no ill of a friend,
nor speak any of an enemy.

Poor Richard's Almanac

Disbelieve two-thirds of the stories
you hear about your neighbors,
and say nothing about the rest.

The Old Farmer's Almanac, 1906

Friendship is a plant of slow growth,
and must undergo and withstand the shocks
of adversity before it is entitled
to the appellation.

George Washington

When you're good to others,
you are best to yourself.

Poor Richard's Almanac

Life is short, but there is always time
for courtesy.

Ralph Waldo Emerson

There is nothing that costs so little
nor goes so far as courtesy.

Old-Time Saying

Keep your words soft and sweet. You never
know when you might have to eat them.

Jerry Clower

Neighbors

Charity is a thing that begins at home
and usually stays there.

Elbert Hubbard

No man is more cheated than the selfish man.

Henry Ward Beecher

Actions, not words, are the true criterion
of the attachment of friends.

George Washington

What is serving God? 'Tis doing good to man.

Poor Richard's Almanac

If you would reap praise, you must sow
the seeds — gentle words and useful deeds.

Poor Richard's Almanac

An ounce of help is worth a pound of pity.

Old-Time Saying

A friend may well be reckoned
the masterpiece of nature.

Ralph Waldo Emerson

Wink at small faults; remember thou hast
great ones.

Poor Richard's Almanac

A spoonful of honey will catch more flies
than a gallon of vinegar.

Poor Richard's Almanac

The best way to cheer yourself up
is to cheer up somebody else.

Mark Twain

Never take away hope from any human being.

Oliver Wendell Holmes, Sr.

A man is known by the company he keeps.
Old-Time Saying

The talk in a country store is known
to be good — sage, amusing, colorful,
and rich in its perception of human nature.
John Kenneth Galbraith

I've always belonged to some quiltin' club
or church bee. When I was raising my kids,
the club was always my time to get off
and get some relief.
Unidentified Quilter

Christmas spirit in a big city is often mixed
with a certain essence of sadness,
but in the country, the peace and goodness
of the season is overwhelming.
Eric Sloane

Search others for their virtues,
thyself for thy vices.
Poor Richard's Almanac

Fish and visitors stink in three days.
Poor Richard's Almanac

Love thy neighbor,
but don't pull down your hedge.
Poor Richard's Almanac

7

Attitude

Henry Ward Beecher remarked, "The difference between perseverance and obstinacy is that one comes from a strong will, and the other comes from a strong won't." For country folk, a strong will comes in handy because life on the farm is seldom easy. What's required is positive thinking and lots of it.

If you find yourself overwhelmed by a strong sense of "won't," think again. And consider the quotations that follow.

The pessimist sees the difficulty in every opportunity; the optimist sees the opportunity in every difficulty.

Lawrence Pearsall Jacks

Life is what we make it.
Always has been.
Always will be.

Grandma Moses

Most people are about as happy
as they make up their minds to be.
Abraham Lincoln

Some men storm imaginary Alps all their
lives and die in the foothills cursing
difficulties which do not exist.
Edgar Watson Howe

I am an old man and have known
a great many troubles, but most of them
never happened.
Mark Twain

Hope of gain lessens pain.
Poor Richard's Almanac

You can't keep the birds from flying
over your head, but you can keep them
from building a nest in your hair.
Old-Time Saying

The fault-finder will find faults
even in paradise.

Henry David Thoreau

Some people know the price of everything
and the value of nothing.

Old-Time Saying

Keep away from people who try to belittle
your ambitions.

Mark Twain

Great hopes make great men.

Thomas Fuller

When a man is angry, he opens his mouth
and shuts his eyes.

Old-Time Saying

Anger improves nothing but the arch
of a cat's back.

Old-Time Saying

Anger profits nobody.

Old-Time Saying

Anger dies quickly in a good man.

Old-Time Saying

Humility makes great men twice honorable.

Poor Richard's Almanac

A big head means a big headache.

Old-Time Saying

He that falls in love with himself
will have no rivals.

Poor Richard's Almanac

Mirth is God's medicine.
Everybody ought to bathe in it.
Henry Ward Beecher

Humor makes all things tolerable.
Henry Ward Beecher

So it is of cheerfulness: The more it is spent,
the more of it remains.
Ralph Waldo Emerson

What is required is sight and insight — then you might add one more: excite.

Robert Frost

This is the day which the Lord hath made; we will rejoice and be glad in it.

Psalms 118: 24

8

Action

A farm is no place for the perpetual procrastinator. In the country, one quickly learns that timing is everything. Unfortunately, it seems that the best time to do most things on a farm is now — if not sooner.

The farmer must operate on Mother Nature's timetable, not his own. As one dairyman observed, "You can't milk cows when *you* feel like it. You've got to milk 'em when *they* feel like it."

The quotations in this chapter attest to the benefits of "getting it done now." Elbert Hubbard wrote, "An ounce of performance is worth more than a pound of preaching." Amen to that.

All the beautiful
sentiments in the world
weigh less than a single
lovely action.

James Russell Lowell

Make the most of yourself,
for that's all there is of you.

Ralph Waldo Emerson

Lost time is never found again.

Poor Richard's Almanac

The most important history is the history
we make today.

Henry Ford

Put in the plow and plant the great hereafter
in the now.

Robert Browning

Make hay while the sun shines.

Old-Time Saying

To escape criticism, do nothing, say nothing, be nothing.

Elbert Hubbard

Thought is the blossom; language the bud; action the fruit.

Ralph Waldo Emerson

You can't escape the responsibility of tomorrow by evading it today.

Abraham Lincoln

Most people spend more time and energy going around problems than trying to solve them.

Henry Ford

Do the thing you fear, and the death of fear is certain.

Ralph Waldo Emerson

Every noble activity makes room for itself.

Ralph Waldo Emerson

Lift where you stand.

Edward Everett Hale

You can't build a reputation
          on what you're going to do.

Henry Ford

Don't sit around and talk about
          what you are going to do — do it.

Old-Time Saying

The shortest answer is doing.

George Herbert

Successful people do what failures
put off until tomorrow.

Old-Time Saying

Nobody's gonna live for you.

Dolly Parton

A man, like a watch,
is to be valued for his going.

William Penn

There is no failure
except in no longer trying.

Elbert Hubbard

When you blunder, blunder forward.

Thomas Edison

Everywhere in life, the true question is
    not what we gain, but what we do.
                                    Thomas Carlyle

It ain't braggin' if you can do it.
                                    Dizzy Dean

If you'd have it done, go; if not, send.
                                    Poor Richard's Almanac

How you start is how you finish.
                                    Old-Time Saying

One today is worth two tomorrows.
                                    Ben Franklin

I leave this rule for others when I'm dead. Be always sure you're right — then go ahead.

Davy Crockett

Strike while the iron is hot.

Old-Time Saying

Action is worry's worst enemy.

Old-Time Saying

Do a thing and be done with it.

Old-Time Saying

Well begun is half done.

Old-Time Saying

Actions speak louder than words,
but not nearly as often.

Old-Time Saying

He started to sing
as he tackled the thing
that couldn't be done,
and he did it.

Edgar A. Guest

9

Character

As long as we have breath, the job of character-building remains unfinished. Because life is punctuated by periods of hardship, humans are continually tested. During tough times, we can either give up or grow up.

It has been said that character, like embroidery, is made stitch by stitch. As you weave the tapestry of your own life, consider the following quotations. And remember that as ye sew, so shall ye reap.

Shallow men believe in luck. Strong men believe in cause and effect.

Ralph Waldo Emerson

Fate is character.

William Winter

If a principle is worth anything,
it is worth living up to.

Ben Franklin

Expedients are for the hour;
principles for the ages.

Henry Ward Beecher

Character is what you are in the dark.

Dwight L. Moody

Character is the result of two things —
mental attitude and the way we spend
our time.

Elbert Hubbard

Character is higher than intellect.

Ralph Waldo Emerson

A clear conscience is a good pillow.

Old-Time Saying

Character is easier kept than recovered.

Thomas Paine

What people say behind your back
is your standing in the community.

Edgar Watson Howe

If I take care of my character, my reputation
will take care of itself.

Dwight L. Moody

Show class, have pride, and display character.
If you do, winning takes care of itself.

Bear Bryant

N ever take the counsel of your fears.

Andrew Jackson

C ourage can achieve everything.

Sam Houston

P ray not for safety from danger,
    but for deliverance from fear.

Ralph Waldo Emerson

K eep conscience clear, then never fear.

Poor Richard's Almanac

What a new face courage puts on everything!

Ralph Waldo Emerson

The thing we fear we bring to pass.

Elbert Hubbard

Courage is always safer than cowardice.

Old-Time Saying

God will not look you over for medals,
degrees or diplomas, but for scars.

Elbert Hubbard

A good man is seldom uneasy,
an ill one never easy.
Poor Richard's Almanac

No man has a good enough memory
to be a successful liar.
Abraham Lincoln

Half the truth is often a great lie.
Poor Richard's Almanac

The rotten apple spoils his companion.
Poor Richard's Almanac

If you lie down with dogs,
you get up with fleas.
Old-Time Saying

The devil sweetens poison with honey.

Poor Richard's Almanac

The devil never sleeps.

Old-Time Saying

You can kill the devil by kindness.

Old-Time Saying

Avoid evil and it will avoid you.

Old-Time Saying

A good example is the best sermon.

Poor Richard's Almanac

<u>10</u>

Behavior

It is said that good behavior is its own reward. Unfortunately, we human beings seem compelled to test the validity of this proposition — with predictable results. Whether we're nine or ninety, misbehavior carries a hefty price tag. Ben Franklin wrote, "If the rascals knew the advantages of virtue, they would become honest."

In this chapter, wise men and women discuss the advantages of virtue. Honesty is not only the best policy, it is also the best *insurance* policy against trouble; plus, the premiums are free and the dividends last a lifetime.

A man cannot be comfortable
without his own approval.

Mark Twain

A clear conscience is a continual Christmas.

Ben Franklin

There is nothing worth being dishonest.

The Old Farmer's Almanac, 1841

The best prosperity consists in doing right.

Lyman Abbott

Whatsoever a man soweth,
that shall he also reap.

Galatians 6: 7

God is better served in resisting a temptation
to evil than in many formal prayers.

William Penn

The reason the way of the transgressor
is hard is because it's so crowded.

Kin Hubbard

'Tis easier to prevent bad habits
than to break them.

Poor Richard's Almanac

One vice adds fuel to another.

The Old Farmer's Almanac, 1841

Behavior

It is easier to stay out than to get out.

Mark Twain

Think of three things — whence you came,
where you are going, and to whom
you must account.

Poor Richard's Almanac

By their fruits ye shall know them.

Matthew 7: 20

He who keeps company with the wolf
will learn to howl.

The Old Farmer's Almanac, 1797

The reward of a good deed is to have done it.

Elbert Hubbard

If you tell the truth, you don't have
to remember what you said.

Mark Twain

If you wish to see the best in others,
    show the best of yourself.

Old-Time Saying

What you *are* thunders so loudly that
I cannot hear what you say to the contrary.

Ralph Waldo Emerson

When men speak ill of thee,
    live so that nobody will believe them.

The Old Farmer's Almanac, 1832

Virtue will not always make a face handsome,
    but vice will certainly make it ugly.

Poor Richard's Almanac

Pretty is as pretty does.

Old-Time Saying

We are not punished for our sins, but by them.

Elbert Hubbard

11

Hard Work

Farm life and laziness don't mix. In the country, there's always plenty of work to do, but never quite enough time to do it. Furthermore, Mother Nature keeps an ever-changing list of unending chores to ensure that the job is never quite finished.

Cyrus Curtis correctly observed, "If you believe in the Lord, He will do half the work — the last half." For a few tips on the first half, turn the page.

Àbout the only thing on a farm that has
an easy time is the dog.

Edgar Watson Howe

A lot of people do not recognize opportunity
because it usually goes around wearing
overalls and looking like hard work.

Thomas Edison

He that does not work shall not eat.

John Smith

Even if a farmer intends to loaf, he gets up
in time to get an early start.

Edgar Watson Howe

Pray for a good harvest, but continue to hoe.

Old-Time Saying

Plough deep while sluggards sleep; and you shall have corn to sell and to keep.

Ben Franklin

He who waits upon fortune
        is never sure of dinner.

Ben Franklin

Keep your nose to the grindstone.

Old-Time Saying

The best helping hand is at the end
        of your sleeve.

Old-Time Saying

If you don't help yourself, nobody will.

Old-Time Saying

Every person should paddle his own boat.

Old-Time Saying

The two kinds of people on earth are
the people who lift and the people who lean.

Ella Wheeler Wilcox

Never trouble another
for what you can do yourself.

Thomas Jefferson

Constant effort and frequent mistakes
are the stepping stones of genius.

Elbert Hubbard

Patience and diligence, like faith,
move mountains.

William Penn

Idle hands are the devil's workshop.

Old-Time Saying

When troubles arise, wise men
go to their work.

Elbert Hubbard

Genius is one percent inspiration and
ninety-nine percent perspiration.

Thomas Edison

Discontent is want of self-reliance.

Ralph Waldo Emerson

Laziness is like money — the more of it
you have, the more you want.

Josh Billings

God helps them that help themselves.

Poor Richard's Almanac

Get happiness out of your work,
   or you may never know what happiness is.
                                    Elbert Hubbard

Love what you do or do something else.
                                    Conway Twitty

Blessed is the man who has found his work.
                                    Elbert Hubbard

Whatsoever thy hand findeth to do,
            do it with thy might.
                                    Ecclesiastes 9: 10

Hard Work

Though the wide universe is full of good;
no kernel of nourishing corn can come to him
but through his toil bestowed on that plot
of ground which is given to him to till.

Ralph Waldo Emerson

Work:
1. That which keeps us out of trouble.
2. A plan of God to circumvent the devil.

Elbert Hubbard

When a man is tired from scything,
he is pleasantly fatigued all over;
when he rests, he rests all over.

Eric Sloane

Some of my best thinking was done
when working hardest at splitting rails.

Abraham Lincoln

The highest reward for man's toil is not what
he gets for it but what he becomes by it.

John Ruskin

Sloth makes all things difficult,
      but industry all things easy.

Ben Franklin

I see no virtues where I smell no sweat.

Francis Quarles, 1640

Don't overwork a willing horse.

Old-Time Saying

Be different, stand out,
      and work your butt off.

Reba McEntire

Little strokes fell great oaks.

Poor Richard's Almanac

Laziness travels so slowly that poverty
soon overtakes him.

Poor Richard's Almanac

Industry need not wish.

Poor Richard's Almanac

Diligence is the mother of good luck.

Poor Richard's Almanac

Well done is twice done.

Poor Richard's Almanac

If you would have
a faithful servant,
serve yourself.

Poor Richard's Almanac

Things may come
to those who wait, but
only the things left by
those who hustle.

Abraham Lincoln

12

Money

In Poor Richard's Almanac, Ben Franklin wrote, "Light purse, heavy heart." Old Ben understood that while money can't buy happiness, neither can poverty.

The following pages contain timeless financial advice designed to keep the bill collector far from your door. If you heed these words, you'll lighten your heart; if you ignore them, you'll pay — in more ways than one.

Common sense dictates that we live comfortably within our means. No wonder. The Poor House is a poor house to call home.

A country merchant advertised various
commodities for sale and gave notice that
he would take in payment all kinds
of country produce except promises.

The Old Farmer's Almanac, 1804

A man in debt is so far a slave.

Ralph Waldo Emerson

Money doesn't grow on trees.

Old-Time Saying

A penny saved is a penny earned.

Ben Franklin

Take care of your pennies and the dollars
will take care of themselves.

Old-Time Saying

Never spend your money before you have it.

Thomas Jefferson

Money is a terrible master but an excellent servant.

P. T. Barnum

Debt is like any other trap — easy enough to get into, but hard enough to get out of.

Josh Billings

Rather go to bed supperless
than rise in debt.

Poor Richard's Almanac

The second vice is lying; the first is debt.

Poor Richard's Almanac

A church debt is the devil's salary.

Henry Ward Beecher

It is hard to pay for bread
that has been eaten.

Old-Time Saying

Money

Who is rich? He that rejoices in his portion.

Poor Richard's Almanac

Never buy what you do not want
because it is cheap.

Thomas Jefferson

Pay what you owe, and you'll know
what's your own.

Poor Richard's Almanac

The holy passion of friendship is of so sweet
and steady and loyal and enduring a nature
that it will last through a whole lifetime,
if not asked to borrow money.

Mark Twain

Don't borrow or lend;
but if you must do one, lend.

Josh Billings

Charity begins at home.

Old-Time Saying

Make all you can, save all you can,
   give all you can.

Old-Time Saying

Beware of little expenses; a small leak
   will sink a great ship.

Ben Franklin

Enough is as good as a feast.

Old-Time Saying

If you desire many things, many things
   will seem but a few.

Poor Richard's Almanac

He that goes a-borrowing goes a-sorrowing.

Ben Franklin

13

Adversity

The veteran farmer is no stranger to adversity. On a farm, lots of things can go wrong — and often do. As the saying goes, if it's not one thing, it's another. Especially in the country.

Herein, we consider some old-fashioned remedies for adversity. These quotations remind us that the secret to surviving tough times is to be *tougher* than the times.

Country people depend
upon two things
for their living: the sky
and the earth. The one
is unpredictable;
the other is reluctant.

C. L. Sonnichsen

What is defeat? Nothing but education,
nothing but the first step to something better.
Wendell Phillips

The greatest test of courage on earth
is to bear defeat without losing heart.
Robert Ingersoll

Our greatest weakness lies in giving up.
The most certain way to succeed is to always
try just one more time.
Thomas Edison

The anvil lasts longer than the hammer.
Old-Time Saying

Failure is the path of least persistence.
Old-Time Saying

Nature, when she adds brains, adds difficulty.

Ralph Waldo Emerson

The proverbial wolf at the door had a litter
of pups on my back porch.

Red Foley

Though misfortune may make a man
unhappy, she can never make him
completely and inseparably miserable
without his own consent.

The Old Farmer's Almanac, 1800

I'll say this for adversity:
People seem to be able to stand it, and that's
more that I can say for prosperity.

Kin Hubbard

God asks no man whether he will accept life.
That is not the choice. You *must* take it.
The only choice is *how*.

Henry Ward Beecher

Difficulties are God's errands and trainers,
and only through them can one come
to the fullness of humanity.

Henry Ward Beecher

Bad times have a scientific value. These are
occasions a good learner would not miss.

Ralph Waldo Emerson

Men see clearer in times of adversity.
Storms purify the atmosphere.

Henry Ward Beecher

Adversity is the stuff that shows whether
you are what you thought you were.

Old-Time Saying

When life kicks you, let it kick you forward.

E. Stanley Jones

Having been poor is no shame,
 but being ashamed of it is.

Poor Richard's Almanac

I was *blessed* with humble beginnings.

Dolly Parton

Success isn't measured by the position
 you reach in life; it's measured
 by the obstacles you overcome.

Booker T. Washington

As the flint contains the spark, unknown
to itself, which the steel alone can awaken to
life, so adversity often reveals to us hidden
gems, which prosperity or negligence
would forever have hidden.

Josh Billings

If you want the rainbow,
you've got to put up
with a little rain.

Dolly Parton

You'll never miss the water
till the well runs dry.

W. C. Handy

I love the man that can smile in trouble,
that can gather strength from distress,
and grow brave by reflection.

Thomas Paine

No gains without pains.

Poor Richard's Almanac

I walk slowly, but I never walk backwards.

Abraham Lincoln

There is no great achievement that is not
the result of patient working and waiting.

J. G. Holland

Better the fruit lost than the tree.

Old-Time Saying

Time is an herb that cures all diseases.

Poor Richard's Almanac

Whatever is is best.

Ella Wheeler Wilcox

Our real blessings often appear to us in the shape of pains, losses, and disappointments; but let us have patience, and we shall soon see them in the proper figures.

Joseph Addison

Not failure, but low aim, is the crime.

James Russell Lowell

When they say it can't
be done, remember
that it can.

Col. Tom Parker

14

Observations on Country Roads, Country Boys, and Other Such Fixtures of Life

We conclude with a potpourri of old-time country wisdom. Enjoy.

The best things in life are free.

Old-Time Saying

There's no accountin' for taste.

Old-Time Saying

Health is the best wealth.

Old-Time Saying

Seeing is believing.

Old-Time Saying

Even a blind hog finds an acorn
every once in a while.

Old-Time Saying

When in doubt,
tell the truth.

Mark Twain

If it ain't broke, don't fix it.

Old-Time Saying

Measure twice, cut once.

Old-Time Saying

One man's trash is another man's treasure.

Old-Time Saying

The dinner bell is always in tune.

Old-Time Saying

You can't get blood from a turnip.

Old-Time Saying

Conscience: an inner voice that warns us someone is looking.

H. L. Mencken

Cleanliness is next to godliness.

Old-Time Saying

An apple never falls far from the tree.

Old-Time Saying

Don't look a gift horse in the mouth.

Old-Time Saying

Don't shut the barn door
after the horse is gone.

Old-Time Saying

Half a loaf is better than none.

Old-Time Saying

Pride goeth before a fall.

Old-Time Saying

A bad penny always comes back.

Old-Time Saying

Mighty oaks from little acorns grow.

Old-Time Saying

If you're lucky, even your rooster
will lay eggs.

Old-Time Saying

The third time is charmed.

Old-Time Saying

Endeavor to live so that
when you die, even the
undertaker will be sorry.

Mark Twain

It is much easier to repent
of the sins we have
already committed
than to repent of those
we intend to commit.

Josh Billings

Eat to live, and not live to eat.
Poor Richard's Almanac

We never repent of having eaten too little.
Thomas Jefferson

To lengthen thy life, lessen thy meals.
Poor Richard's Almanac

Necessity never made a good bargain.

Poor Richard's Almanac

A poor excuse is better than none.

Old-Time Saying

Silence is golden.

Old-Time Saying

He that riseth late must trot all day and shall scarce overtake his business at night.

Poor Richard's Almanac

Opportunity knocks once at every man's door and then keeps on knocking.

George Ade

Drive thy business! — let not it drive you.

Poor Richard's Almanac

You can fool some of the people all of the time, and all of the people some of the time, but you cannot fool all of the people all of the time.

Abraham Lincoln

The early morning
has gold in its mouth.

Ben Franklin

"At ease," she said. "Maneuvers begin
when you get those whiskers off your chin."

Burma Shave Road Sign

Take the back roads instead of the highways.

Minnie Pearl

The perfect hostess will see to it that
the works of male and female authors
be properly separated on her bookshelves.

The Old Farmer's Almanac, 1853

Do the common things of life in an uncommon way.

George Washington Carver

You can take a boy
out of the country,
but you can't take the
country out of the boy.

Old-Time Saying

Sources

Sources

1778 Almanac   42

Lyman Abbott   98

Joseph Addison   131

George Ade   58, 144

John Arnold   33

Francis Bacon   41

P. T. Barnum   118

Henry Ward Beecher   26, 50, 62, 67, 74, 90, 119, 126, 127

Josh Billings   (Henry Wheeler Shaw)   15, 19, 20, 24, 27,
    28, 32, 37, 52, 108, 119, 120, 128, 141

Barbara Dodge Borland   45

Richard Briers   45

Lawton Brooks   21

Robert Browning   79

Bear Bryant   91

Horace Bushnell   37

Thomas Carlyle   83

George Washington Carver   147

Jerry Clower   61

Will D. Cobb   27

Mike Cook   24

Calvin Coolidge   47

Davy Crockett   84

Cyrus Curtis   103

Dizzy Dean   83

Andy Devine   55

Thomas Edison   82, 104, 108, 125

Ralph Waldo Emerson   34, 35, 36, 41, 46, 47, 48, 57, 58,
    61, 64, 74, 79, 80, 81, 88, 90, 92, 93, 101, 108, 110,
    116, 126, 127

Farmer's Manual   54

Sources

H. L. Mencken 137
Dwight L. Moody 90, 91
Grandma Moses 69
Thomas Paine 46, 91, 130
Col. Tom Parker 132
Dolly Parton 82, 128, 129
Minnie Pearl 146
William Penn 27, 31, 34, 50, 58, 82, 99, 107
Wendell Phillips 125
James Pickering 54
Poor Richard's Almanac (Ben Franklin) 16, 18, 19, 20,
    22, 24, 25, 26, 27, 28, 29, 36, 40, 51, 52, 54, 58, 60, 61,
    62, 64, 66, 70, 73, 79, 83, 92, 94, 95, 96, 99, 100, 101,
    108, 112, 113, 119, 120, 121, 128, 130, 131, 142, 143,
    144
Francis Quarles 111
Grantland Rice 38
John Ruskin 47, 110
Eric Sloane 46, 65, 110
John Smith 104
C. L. Sonnichsen 124
Dick Syatt 47
The Farmer's Almanac 49
The Old Farmer's Almanac 16, 21, 36, 42, 54, 56, 60, 98,
    99, 100, 101, 116, 126, 146
The Missouri Pharmacist 19
Henry David Thoreau 20, 48, 71
Mark Twain 64, 70, 71, 98, 100, 120, 135, 140
Conway Twitty 109
Henry Vaughan 42
Charles Dudley Warner 42, 43

WG

About the Author

Criswell Freeman is a Doctor of Clinical Psychology living in Nashville, Tennessee. He is the author of *When Life Throws You a Curveball, Hit It* and *The Wisdom Series* from WALNUT GROVE PRESS.

About Wisdom Books

Wisdom Books chronicle memorable quotations in an easy-to-read style. Written by Criswell Freeman, this series provides inspiring, thoughtful and humorous messages from entertainers, athletes, scientists, politicians, clerics, writers and renegades. Each title focuses on a particular region or area of special interest.

Combining his passion for quotations with extensive training in psychology, Dr. Freeman revisits timeless themes such as perseverance, courage, love, forgiveness and faith.

"Quotations help us remember the simple yet profound truths that give life perspective and meaning," notes Freeman. "When it comes to life's most important lessons, we can all use gentle reminders."

The Wisdom Series
by Dr. Criswell Freeman

Regional Titles

Wisdom Made in America	ISBN 1-887655-07-7
The Book of Southern Wisdom	ISBN 0-9640955-3-X
The Wisdom of the Midwest	ISBN 1-887655-17-4
The Wisdom of the West	ISBN 1-887655-31-X
The Book of Texas Wisdom	ISBN 0-9640955-8-0
The Book of Florida Wisdom	ISBN 0-9640955-9-9
The Book of California Wisdom	ISBN 1-887655-14-X
The Book of New York Wisdom	ISBN 1-887655-16-6
The Book of New England Wisdom	ISBN 1-887655-15-8

Sports Titles

The Golfer's Book of Wisdom	ISBN 0-9640955-6-4
The Putter Principle	ISBN 1-887655-39-5
The Golfer's Guide to Life	ISBN 1-887655-38-7
The Wisdom of Southern Football	ISBN 0-9640955-7-2
The Book of Stock Car Wisdom	ISBN 1-887655-12-3
The Wisdom of Old-Time Baseball	ISBN 1-887655-08-5
The Book of Football Wisdom	ISBN 1-887655-18-2
The Book of Basketball Wisdom	ISBN 1-887655-32-8
The Fisherman's Guide to Life	ISBN 1-887655-30-1
The Tennis Lover's Guide to Life	ISBN 1-887655-36-0

Special Interest Titles

The Book of Country Music Wisdom	ISBN 0-9640955-1-3
Old-Time Country Wisdom	ISBN 1-887655-26-3
The Wisdom of Old-Time Television	ISBN 1-887655-64-6
The Cowboy's Guide to Life	ISBN 1-887655-41-7
The Wisdom of the Heart	ISBN 1-887655-34-4
The Guide to Better Birthdays	ISBN 1-887655-35-2
The Gardener's Guide to Life	ISBN 1-887655-40-9
Minutes from the Great Women's Coffee Club (by Angela Beasley)	ISBN 1-887655-33-6

Wisdom Books are available through booksellers everywhere.
For information about a retailer near you, call 1-800-256-8584.